This journal belongs to:

_____

INSERT NAME

OTHER GUIDED JOURNALS & DIARIES
by
KINYATTA E. GRAY

 **I Miss You...**

Daily Writing Prompts for Reflection, Remembrance, and Spirit Renewal

 **I Am A Man. I Have Feelings.**

A Guided 90-Day Self-Reflections & Gratitude Journal for Men

 **Fashionista's Travel Diary**

A Guided Travel Diary for Travel Planning & Reflections

 **The Queen's Manifestation Journal**

Daily Writing Prompt for Manifesting the Life You Want

 **I'm Doing Me**

The Ultimate Breakup Diary for Venting, Reflection & Spirit Renewal

 **Budget & Shop**

A Monthly Personal Budget & Expense Tracker for Young Adults

 **While I'm Still Here**

A Guided Expression Journal of Life, Love and Legacy for Those Preparing to Transition

 **My Life My Love My Truth**

LGBTQ journal

 **My Crazy Teenage Life**

The Ultimate Expression Diary for Venting, Self-Reflections and Self-Love

"THERE IS NO WAY TO BE A PERFECT MOTHER, BUT A MILLION WAYS TO BE A GOOD ONE. "

~Jill Churchill

Sexy Baby Mama
Self-Reflections

Today's Date:
_____

I practiced Self-Care today by:

My support system consists of:

I Feel:

☐ Supported
☐ Protected
☐ Happy
☐ Excited
☐ Optimistic
☐ Overwhelmed
☐ In Love
☐ Sad
☐ Angry
☐ Scared

Self care
Is Not
Selfish

Sexy Baby Mama
Self-Reflections

I practiced Self-Care today by:

My support system consists of:

I Feel:

☐ Supported
☐ Protected
☐ Happy
☐ Excited
☐ Optimistic
☐ Overwhelmed
☐ In Love
☐ Sad
☐ Angry
☐ Scared

Self care
Is Not
Selfish

Sexy Baby Mama
Self-Reflections

I practiced Self-Care today by:

My support system consists of:

I Feel:

- ☐ Supported
- ☐ Protected
- ☐ Happy
- ☐ Excited
- ☐ Optimistic
- ☐ Overwhelmed
- ☐ In Love
- ☐ Sad
- ☐ Angry
- ☐ Scared

Self care
Is Not
Selfish

Sexy Baby Mama
Self-Reflections

I practiced Self-Care today by:

My support system consists of:

I Feel:

☐ Supported
☐ Protected
☐ Happy
☐ Excited
☐ Optimistic
☐ Overwhelmed
☐ In Love
☐ Sad
☐ Angry
☐ Scared

Self care
Is Not
Selfish

Sexy Baby Mama
Self-Reflections

Today's Date:

_____

I practiced Self-Care today by:

My support system consists of:

I Feel:

☐ Supported
☐ Protected
☐ Happy
☐ Excited
☐ Optimistic
☐ Overwhelmed
☐ In Love
☐ Sad
☐ Angry
☐ Scared

Self-care
Is Not
Selfish

Sexy Baby Mama
Self-Reflections

I practiced Self-Care today by:

My support system consists of:

I Feel:

☐ Supported
☐ Protected
☐ Happy
☐ Excited
☐ Optimistic
☐ Overwhelmed
☐ In Love
☐ Sad
☐ Angry
☐ Scared

Self care
Is Not
Selfish

Sexy Baby Mama
Self-Reflections

_____

I practiced Self-Care today by:

My support system consists of:

I Feel:

☐ Supported
☐ Protected
☐ Happy
☐ Excited
☐ Optimistic
☐ Overwhelmed
☐ In Love
☐ Sad
☐ Angry
☐ Scared

_____
_____
_____
_____
_____
_____
_____
_____
_____
_____
_____
_____
_____
_____
_____
_____

Self care
Is Not
Selfish

_____
_____
_____

Sexy Baby Mama
Self-Reflections

_____

I practiced Self-Care today by:

My support system consists of:

I Feel:

- ☐ Supported
- ☐ Protected
- ☐ Happy
- ☐ Excited
- ☐ Optimistic
- ☐ Overwhelmed
- ☐ In Love
- ☐ Sad
- ☐ Angry
- ☐ Scared

Self-care Is Not Selfish

Sexy Baby Mama
Self-Reflections

I practiced Self-Care today by:

My support system consists of:

I Feel:

☐ Supported
☐ Protected
☐ Happy
☐ Excited
☐ Optimistic
☐ Overwhelmed
☐ In Love
☐ Sad
☐ Angry
☐ Scared

Self care
Is Not
Selfish

Sexy Baby Mama
Self-Reflections

_____

I practiced Self-Care today by:

My support system consists of:

I Feel:

☐ Supported
☐ Protected
☐ Happy
☐ Excited
☐ Optimistic
☐ Overwhelmed
☐ In Love
☐ Sad
☐ Angry
☐ Scared

Self care
Is Not
Selfish

Sexy Baby Mama
Self-Reflections

I practiced Self-Care today by:

My support system consists of:

I Feel:

- ☐ Supported
- ☐ Protected
- ☐ Happy
- ☐ Excited
- ☐ Optimistic
- ☐ Overwhelmed
- ☐ In Love
- ☐ Sad
- ☐ Angry
- ☐ Scared

Self care
Is Not
Selfish

Sexy Baby Mama
Self-Reflections

I practiced Self-Care today by:

My support system consists of:

I Feel:

☐ Supported
☐ Protected
☐ Happy
☐ Excited
☐ Optimistic
☐ Overwhelmed
☐ In Love
☐ Sad
☐ Angry
☐ Scared

Self care
Is Not
Selfish

Sexy Baby Mama
Self-Reflections

I practiced Self-Care today by:

My support system consists of:

I Feel:

- ☐ Supported
- ☐ Protected
- ☐ Happy
- ☐ Excited
- ☐ Optimistic
- ☐ Overwhelmed
- ☐ In Love
- ☐ Sad
- ☐ Angry
- ☐ Scared

Self care
Is Not
Selfish

Sexy Baby Mama
Self-Reflections

Today's Date:
_____

I practiced Self-Care today by:

My support system consists of:

I Feel:

☐ Supported
☐ Protected
☐ Happy
☐ Excited
☐ Optimistic
☐ Overwhelmed
☐ In Love
☐ Sad
☐ Angry
☐ Scared

_____

_____

_____

_____

_____

_____

_____

_____

_____

_____

_____

_____

_____

_____

_____

_____

_____

_____

_____

Self-care
Is Not
Selfish

Sexy Baby Mama
Self-Reflections

I practiced Self-Care today by:

My support system consists of:

I Feel:

- ☐ Supported
- ☐ Protected
- ☐ Happy
- ☐ Excited
- ☐ Optimistic
- ☐ Overwhelmed
- ☐ In Love
- ☐ Sad
- ☐ Angry
- ☐ Scared

Self care
Is Not
Selfish

20

Sexy Baby Mama
Self-Reflections

I practiced Self-Care today by:

My support system consists of:

I Feel:

☐ Supported
☐ Protected
☐ Happy
☐ Excited
☐ Optimistic
☐ Overwhelmed
☐ In Love
☐ Sad
☐ Angry
☐ Scared

Self care
Is Not
Selfish

Sexy Baby Mama
Self-Reflections

I practiced Self-Care today by:

My support system consists of:

I Feel:

- ☐ Supported
- ☐ Protected
- ☐ Happy
- ☐ Excited
- ☐ Optimistic
- ☐ Overwhelmed
- ☐ In Love
- ☐ Sad
- ☐ Angry
- ☐ Scared

Self care
Is Not
Selfish

Sexy Baby Mama
Self-Reflections

I practiced Self-Care today by:

My support system consists of:

I Feel:

☐ Supported
☐ Protected
☐ Happy
☐ Excited
☐ Optimistic
☐ Overwhelmed
☐ In Love
☐ Sad
☐ Angry
☐ Scared

Self care
Is Not
Selfish

Sexy Baby Mama
Self-Reflections

I practiced Self-Care today by:

My support system consists of:

I Feel:

- ☐ Supported
- ☐ Protected
- ☐ Happy
- ☐ Excited
- ☐ Optimistic
- ☐ Overwhelmed
- ☐ In Love
- ☐ Sad
- ☐ Angry
- ☐ Scared

Self care
Is Not
Selfish

Sexy Baby Mama
Self-Reflections

I practiced Self-Care today by:

My support system consists of:

I Feel:

- ☐ Supported
- ☐ Protected
- ☐ Happy
- ☐ Excited
- ☐ Optimistic
- ☐ Overwhelmed
- ☐ In Love
- ☐ Sad
- ☐ Angry
- ☐ Scared

Self-care
Is Not
Selfish

Sexy Baby Mama
Self-Reflections

I practiced Self-Care today by:

My support system consists of:

I Feel:

- ☐ Supported
- ☐ Protected
- ☐ Happy
- ☐ Excited
- ☐ Optimistic
- ☐ Overwhelmed
- ☐ In Love
- ☐ Sad
- ☐ Angry
- ☐ Scared

Self care Is Not Selfish

Sexy Baby Mama
Self-Reflections

I practiced Self-Care today by:

My support system consists of:

I Feel:

- ☐ Supported
- ☐ Protected
- ☐ Happy
- ☐ Excited
- ☐ Optimistic
- ☐ Overwhelmed
- ☐ In Love
- ☐ Sad
- ☐ Angry
- ☐ Scared

Self care
Is Not
Selfish

Sexy Baby Mama
Self-Reflections

I practiced Self-Care today by:

My support system consists of:

I Feel:

☐ Supported
☐ Protected
☐ Happy
☐ Excited
☐ Optimistic
☐ Overwhelmed
☐ In Love
☐ Sad
☐ Angry
☐ Scared

Self care
Is Not
Selfish

Sexy Baby Mama
Self-Reflections

I practiced Self-Care today by:

My support system consists of:

I Feel:

☐ Supported
☐ Protected
☐ Happy
☐ Excited
☐ Optimistic
☐ Overwhelmed
☐ In Love
☐ Sad
☐ Angry
☐ Scared

Self care
Is Not
Selfish

Sexy Baby Mama
Self-Reflections

I practiced Self-Care today by:

My support system consists of:

I Feel:

☐ Supported
☐ Protected
☐ Happy
☐ Excited
☐ Optimistic
☐ Overwhelmed
☐ In Love
☐ Sad
☐ Angry
☐ Scared

Self care
Is Not
Selfish

Sexy Baby Mama
Self-Reflections

I practiced Self-Care today by:

My support system consists of:

I Feel:

☐ Supported
☐ Protected
☐ Happy
☐ Excited
☐ Optimistic
☐ Overwhelmed
☐ In Love
☐ Sad
☐ Angry
☐ Scared

Self care
Is Not
Selfish

Sexy Baby Mama
Self-Reflections

I practiced Self-Care today by:

My support system consists of:

I Feel:

- ☐ Supported
- ☐ Protected
- ☐ Happy
- ☐ Excited
- ☐ Optimistic
- ☐ Overwhelmed
- ☐ In Love
- ☐ Sad
- ☐ Angry
- ☐ Scared

Self care
Is Not
Selfish

Sexy Baby Mama
Self-Reflections

I practiced Self-Care today by:

My support system consists of:

I Feel:

- ☐ Supported
- ☐ Protected
- ☐ Happy
- ☐ Excited
- ☐ Optimistic
- ☐ Overwhelmed
- ☐ In Love
- ☐ Sad
- ☐ Angry
- ☐ Scared

Self care
Is Not
Selfish

Sexy Baby Mama
Self-Reflections

Today's Date:
_____

I practiced Self-Care today by:

My support system consists of:

I Feel:

- ☐ Supported
- ☐ Protected
- ☐ Happy
- ☐ Excited
- ☐ Optimistic
- ☐ Overwhelmed
- ☐ In Love
- ☐ Sad
- ☐ Angry
- ☐ Scared

Self-care Is Not Selfish

Sexy Baby Mama
Self-Reflections

I practiced Self-Care today by:

My support system consists of:

I Feel:

☐ Supported
☐ Protected
☐ Happy
☐ Excited
☐ Optimistic
☐ Overwhelmed
☐ In Love
☐ Sad
☐ Angry
☐ Scared

Self care
Is Not
Selfish

Sexy Baby Mama
Self-Reflections

I practiced Self-Care today by:

My support system consists of:

I Feel:

- ☐ Supported
- ☐ Protected
- ☐ Happy
- ☐ Excited
- ☐ Optimistic
- ☐ Overwhelmed
- ☐ In Love
- ☐ Sad
- ☐ Angry
- ☐ Scared

Self care Is Not Selfish

Sexy Baby Mama
Self-Reflections

_____

I practiced Self-Care today by:

My support system consists of:

I Feel:

- ☐ Supported
- ☐ Protected
- ☐ Happy
- ☐ Excited
- ☐ Optimistic
- ☐ Overwhelmed
- ☐ In Love
- ☐ Sad
- ☐ Angry
- ☐ Scared

_____
_____
_____
_____
_____
_____
_____
_____
_____
_____
_____
_____
_____
_____
_____
_____
_____
_____
_____

Self-care
Is Not
Selfish

Sexy Baby Mama
Self-Reflections

_____

I practiced Self-Care today by:

My support system consists of:

I Feel:

☐ Supported
☐ Protected
☐ Happy
☐ Excited
☐ Optimistic
☐ Overwhelmed
☐ In Love
☐ Sad
☐ Angry
☐ Scared

Self care
Is Not
Selfish

Sexy Baby Mama
Self-Reflections

I practiced Self-Care today by:

My support system consists of:

I Feel:

☐ Supported
☐ Protected
☐ Happy
☐ Excited
☐ Optimistic
☐ Overwhelmed
☐ In Love
☐ Sad
☐ Angry
☐ Scared

Self care
Is Not
Selfish

Sexy Baby Mama
Self-Reflections

I practiced Self-Care today by:

My support system consists of:

I Feel:

☐ Supported
☐ Protected
☐ Happy
☐ Excited
☐ Optimistic
☐ Overwhelmed
☐ In Love
☐ Sad
☐ Angry
☐ Scared

Self care
Is Not
Selfish

Sexy Baby Mama
Self-Reflections

I practiced Self-Care today by:

My support system consists of:

I Feel:

☐ Supported
☐ Protected
☐ Happy
☐ Excited
☐ Optimistic
☐ Overwhelmed
☐ In Love
☐ Sad
☐ Angry
☐ Scared

Self care Is Not Selfish

Sexy Baby Mama
Self-Reflections

_____

I practiced Self-Care today by:

My support system consists of:

I Feel:

- ☐ Supported
- ☐ Protected
- ☐ Happy
- ☐ Excited
- ☐ Optimistic
- ☐ Overwhelmed
- ☐ In Love
- ☐ Sad
- ☐ Angry
- ☐ Scared

_____

_____

_____

_____

_____

_____

_____

_____

_____

_____

_____

_____

_____

_____

_____

_____

_____

Self care
Is Not
Selfish

Sexy Baby Mama
Self-Reflections

I practiced Self-Care today by:

My support system consists of:

I Feel:

☐ Supported
☐ Protected
☐ Happy
☐ Excited
☐ Optimistic
☐ Overwhelmed
☐ In Love
☐ Sad
☐ Angry
☐ Scared

Self care
Is Not
Selfish

Sexy Baby Mama
Self-Reflections

I practiced Self-Care today by:

My support system consists of:

I Feel:

- ☐ Supported
- ☐ Protected
- ☐ Happy
- ☐ Excited
- ☐ Optimistic
- ☐ Overwhelmed
- ☐ In Love
- ☐ Sad
- ☐ Angry
- ☐ Scared

Self care
Is Not
Selfish

Sexy Baby Mama
Self-Reflections

I practiced Self-Care today by:

My support system consists of:

I Feel:

☐ Supported
☐ Protected
☐ Happy
☐ Excited
☐ Optimistic
☐ Overwhelmed
☐ In Love
☐ Sad
☐ Angry
☐ Scared

Self care
Is Not
Selfish

Sexy Baby Mama
Self-Reflections

I practiced Self-Care today by:

My support system consists of:

I Feel:

- ☐ Supported
- ☐ Protected
- ☐ Happy
- ☐ Excited
- ☐ Optimistic
- ☐ Overwhelmed
- ☐ In Love
- ☐ Sad
- ☐ Angry
- ☐ Scared

Self care
Is Not
Selfish

Sexy Baby Mama
Self-Reflections

_____

I practiced Self-Care today by:

My support system consists of:

I Feel:

☐ Supported
☐ Protected
☐ Happy
☐ Excited
☐ Optimistic
☐ Overwhelmed
☐ In Love
☐ Sad
☐ Angry
☐ Scared

_____

_____

_____

_____

_____

_____

_____

_____

_____

_____

_____

_____

_____

_____

_____

_____

_____

_____

_____

Self care
Is Not
Selfish

Sexy Baby Mama
Self-Reflections

I practiced Self-Care today by:

My support system consists of:

I Feel:

☐ Supported
☐ Protected
☐ Happy
☐ Excited
☐ Optimistic
☐ Overwhelmed
☐ In Love
☐ Sad
☐ Angry
☐ Scared

_____
_____
_____
_____
_____
_____
_____
_____
_____
_____
_____
_____
_____
_____
_____
_____
_____
_____

Self care Is Not Selfish

48

Sexy Baby Mama
Self-Reflections

I practiced Self-Care today by:

My support system consists of:

I Feel:

☐ Supported
☐ Protected
☐ Happy
☐ Excited
☐ Optimistic
☐ Overwhelmed
☐ In Love
☐ Sad
☐ Angry
☐ Scared

Self care
Is Not
Selfish

Sexy Baby Mama
Self-Reflections

I practiced Self-Care today by:

My support system consists of:

I Feel:

☐ Supported
☐ Protected
☐ Happy
☐ Excited
☐ Optimistic
☐ Overwhelmed
☐ In Love
☐ Sad
☐ Angry
☐ Scared

Self care
Is Not
Selfish

Sexy Baby Mama
Self-Reflections

I practiced Self-Care today by:

My support system consists of:

I Feel:

☐ Supported
☐ Protected
☐ Happy
☐ Excited
☐ Optimistic
☐ Overwhelmed
☐ In Love
☐ Sad
☐ Angry
☐ Scared

Self care
Is Not
Selfish

Sexy Baby Mama
Self-Reflections

I practiced Self-Care today by:

My support system consists of:

I Feel:

- ☐ Supported
- ☐ Protected
- ☐ Happy
- ☐ Excited
- ☐ Optimistic
- ☐ Overwhelmed
- ☐ In Love
- ☐ Sad
- ☐ Angry
- ☐ Scared

Self care
Is Not
Selfish

Sexy Baby Mama
Self-Reflections

I practiced Self-Care today by:

My support system consists of:

I Feel:

☐ Supported
☐ Protected
☐ Happy
☐ Excited
☐ Optimistic
☐ Overwhelmed
☐ In Love
☐ Sad
☐ Angry
☐ Scared

Self care
Is Not
Selfish

Sexy Baby Mama
Self-Reflections

I practiced Self-Care today by:

My support system consists of:

I Feel:

- ☐ Supported
- ☐ Protected
- ☐ Happy
- ☐ Excited
- ☐ Optimistic
- ☐ Overwhelmed
- ☐ In Love
- ☐ Sad
- ☐ Angry
- ☐ Scared

Self care Is Not Selfish

Sexy Baby Mama
Self-Reflections

I practiced Self-Care today by:

My support system consists of:

I Feel:

☐ Supported
☐ Protected
☐ Happy
☐ Excited
☐ Optimistic
☐ Overwhelmed
☐ In Love
☐ Sad
☐ Angry
☐ Scared

Self care
Is Not
Selfish

Sexy Baby Mama
Self-Reflections

_____

I practiced Self-Care today by:

My support system consists of:

I Feel:

☐ Supported
☐ Protected
☐ Happy
☐ Excited
☐ Optimistic
☐ Overwhelmed
☐ In Love
☐ Sad
☐ Angry
☐ Scared

Self care
Is Not
Selfish

Sexy Baby Mama
Self-Reflections

I practiced Self-Care today by:

My support system consists of:

I Feel:

- ☐ Supported
- ☐ Protected
- ☐ Happy
- ☐ Excited
- ☐ Optimistic
- ☐ Overwhelmed
- ☐ In Love
- ☐ Sad
- ☐ Angry
- ☐ Scared

Self care
Is Not
Selfish

Sexy Baby Mama
Self-Reflections

Today's Date:
_____

I practiced Self-Care today by:

My support system consists of:

I Feel:

- ☐ Supported
- ☐ Protected
- ☐ Happy
- ☐ Excited
- ☐ Optimistic
- ☐ Overwhelmed
- ☐ In Love
- ☐ Sad
- ☐ Angry
- ☐ Scared

Self care
Is Not
Selfish

Sexy Baby Mama
Self-Reflections

I practiced Self-Care today by:

My support system consists of:

I Feel:

☐ Supported
☐ Protected
☐ Happy
☐ Excited
☐ Optimistic
☐ Overwhelmed
☐ In Love
☐ Sad
☐ Angry
☐ Scared

Self care
Is Not
Selfish

Sexy Baby Mama
Self-Reflections

I practiced Self-Care today by:

My support system consists of:

I Feel:

☐ Supported
☐ Protected
☐ Happy
☐ Excited
☐ Optimistic
☐ Overwhelmed
☐ In Love
☐ Sad
☐ Angry
☐ Scared

Self care
Is Not
Selfish

Sexy Baby Mama
Self-Reflections

Flights in Stilettos

Today's Date:
_____

I practiced Self-Care today by:

My support system consists of:

I Feel:

☐ Supported
☐ Protected
☐ Happy
☐ Excited
☐ Optimistic
☐ Overwhelmed
☐ In Love
☐ Sad
☐ Angry
☐ Scared

Self-care Is Not Selfish

Sexy Baby Mama
Self-Reflections

Today's Date:

I practiced Self-Care today by:

My support system consists of:

I Feel:

☐ Supported
☐ Protected
☐ Happy
☐ Excited
☐ Optimistic
☐ Overwhelmed
☐ In Love
☐ Sad
☐ Angry
☐ Scared

Self care
Is Not
Selfish

62

Sexy Baby Mama
Self-Reflections

I practiced Self-Care today by:

My support system consists of:

I Feel:

☐ Supported
☐ Protected
☐ Happy
☐ Excited
☐ Optimistic
☐ Overwhelmed
☐ In Love
☐ Sad
☐ Angry
☐ Scared

_____

_____

_____

_____

_____

_____

_____

_____

_____

_____

_____

_____

_____

_____

_____

_____

_____

_____

_____

Self care
Is Not
Selfish

Sexy Baby Mama
Self-Reflections

I practiced Self-Care today by:

My support system consists of:

I Feel:

☐ Supported
☐ Protected
☐ Happy
☐ Excited
☐ Optimistic
☐ Overwhelmed
☐ In Love
☐ Sad
☐ Angry
☐ Scared

Self care
Is Not
Selfish

Sexy Baby Mama
Self-Reflections

I practiced Self-Care today by:

My support system consists of:

I Feel:

☐ Supported
☐ Protected
☐ Happy
☐ Excited
☐ Optimistic
☐ Overwhelmed
☐ In Love
☐ Sad
☐ Angry
☐ Scared

Self care
Is Not
Selfish

Sexy Baby Mama
Self-Reflections

I practiced Self-Care today by:

My support system consists of:

I Feel:

- ☐ Supported
- ☐ Protected
- ☐ Happy
- ☐ Excited
- ☐ Optimistic
- ☐ Overwhelmed
- ☐ In Love
- ☐ Sad
- ☐ Angry
- ☐ Scared

Self care
Is Not
Selfish

Sexy Baby Mama
Self-Reflections

I practiced Self-Care today by:

My support system consists of:

I Feel:

☐ Supported
☐ Protected
☐ Happy
☐ Excited
☐ Optimistic
☐ Overwhelmed
☐ In Love
☐ Sad
☐ Angry
☐ Scared

Self care Is Not Selfish

Sexy Baby Mama
Self-Reflections

I practiced Self-Care today by:

My support system consists of:

I Feel:

☐ Supported
☐ Protected
☐ Happy
☐ Excited
☐ Optimistic
☐ Overwhelmed
☐ In Love
☐ Sad
☐ Angry
☐ Scared

Self care Is Not Selfish

Sexy Baby Mama
Self-Reflections

I practiced Self-Care today by:

My support system consists of:

I Feel:

☐ Supported
☐ Protected
☐ Happy
☐ Excited
☐ Optimistic
☐ Overwhelmed
☐ In Love
☐ Sad
☐ Angry
☐ Scared

Self care
Is Not
Selfish

Sexy Baby Mama
Self-Reflections

I practiced Self-Care today by:

My support system consists of:

I Feel:

☐ Supported
☐ Protected
☐ Happy
☐ Excited
☐ Optimistic
☐ Overwhelmed
☐ In Love
☐ Sad
☐ Angry
☐ Scared

Self care
Is Not
Selfish

Sexy Baby Mama
Self-Reflections

I practiced Self-Care today by:

My support system consists of:

I Feel:

☐ Supported
☐ Protected
☐ Happy
☐ Excited
☐ Optimistic
☐ Overwhelmed
☐ In Love
☐ Sad
☐ Angry
☐ Scared

Self care
Is Not
Selfish

Sexy Baby Mama
Self-Reflections

I practiced Self-Care today by:

My support system consists of:

I Feel:

☐ Supported
☐ Protected
☐ Happy
☐ Excited
☐ Optimistic
☐ Overwhelmed
☐ In Love
☐ Sad
☐ Angry
☐ Scared

Self care
Is Not
Selfish

Sexy Baby Mama
Self-Reflections

Today's Date:
_____

I practiced Self-Care today by:

My support system consists of:

I Feel:

- ☐ Supported
- ☐ Protected
- ☐ Happy
- ☐ Excited
- ☐ Optimistic
- ☐ Overwhelmed
- ☐ In Love
- ☐ Sad
- ☐ Angry
- ☐ Scared

Self care
Is Not
Selfish

Sexy Baby Mama
Self-Reflections

_____

I practiced Self-Care today by:

My support system consists of:

I Feel:

☐ Supported
☐ Protected
☐ Happy
☐ Excited
☐ Optimistic
☐ Overwhelmed
☐ In Love
☐ Sad
☐ Angry
☐ Scared

_____
_____
_____
_____
_____
_____
_____
_____
_____
_____
_____
_____
_____
_____
_____
_____
_____
_____
_____

Self care
Is Not
Selfish

Sexy Baby Mama
Self-Reflections

Today's Date:

_____

I practiced Self-Care today by:

My support system consists of:

I Feel:

- ☐ Supported
- ☐ Protected
- ☐ Happy
- ☐ Excited
- ☐ Optimistic
- ☐ Overwhelmed
- ☐ In Love
- ☐ Sad
- ☐ Angry
- ☐ Scared

Self care
Is Not
Selfish

Sexy Baby Mama
Self-Reflections

Today's Date:
_____

I practiced Self-Care today by:

My support system consists of:

I Feel:

- ☐ Supported
- ☐ Protected
- ☐ Happy
- ☐ Excited
- ☐ Optimistic
- ☐ Overwhelmed
- ☐ In Love
- ☐ Sad
- ☐ Angry
- ☐ Scared

Self care
Is Not
Selfish

Sexy Baby Mama
Self-Reflections

I practiced Self-Care today by:

My support system consists of:

I Feel:

☐ Supported
☐ Protected
☐ Happy
☐ Excited
☐ Optimistic
☐ Overwhelmed
☐ In Love
☐ Sad
☐ Angry
☐ Scared

Self care
Is Not
Selfish

Sexy Baby Mama
Self-Reflections

I practiced Self-Care today by:

My support system consists of:

I Feel:

- ☐ Supported
- ☐ Protected
- ☐ Happy
- ☐ Excited
- ☐ Optimistic
- ☐ Overwhelmed
- ☐ In Love
- ☐ Sad
- ☐ Angry
- ☐ Scared

Self care
Is Not
Selfish

Sexy Baby Mama
Self-Reflections

I practiced Self-Care today by:

My support system consists of:

I Feel:

☐ Supported
☐ Protected
☐ Happy
☐ Excited
☐ Optimistic
☐ Overwhelmed
☐ In Love
☐ Sad
☐ Angry
☐ Scared

Self care
Is Not
Selfish

Sexy Baby Mama
Self-Reflections

_____

I practiced Self-Care today by:

My support system consists of:

I Feel:

- ☐ Supported
- ☐ Protected
- ☐ Happy
- ☐ Excited
- ☐ Optimistic
- ☐ Overwhelmed
- ☐ In Love
- ☐ Sad
- ☐ Angry
- ☐ Scared

Self-care Is Not Selfish

Sexy Baby Mama
Self-Reflections

I practiced Self-Care today by:

My support system consists of:

I Feel:

- ☐ Supported
- ☐ Protected
- ☐ Happy
- ☐ Excited
- ☐ Optimistic
- ☐ Overwhelmed
- ☐ In Love
- ☐ Sad
- ☐ Angry
- ☐ Scared

Self care
Is Not
Selfish

Sexy Baby Mama
Self-Reflections

I practiced Self-Care today by:

My support system consists of:

I Feel:

- ☐ Supported
- ☐ Protected
- ☐ Happy
- ☐ Excited
- ☐ Optimistic
- ☐ Overwhelmed
- ☐ In Love
- ☐ Sad
- ☐ Angry
- ☐ Scared

Self care
Is Not
Selfish

Sexy Baby Mama
Self-Reflections

_____

I practiced Self-Care today by:

My support system consists of:

I Feel:

☐ Supported
☐ Protected
☐ Happy
☐ Excited
☐ Optimistic
☐ Overwhelmed
☐ In Love
☐ Sad
☐ Angry
☐ Scared

_____

_____

_____

_____

_____

_____

_____

_____

_____

_____

_____

_____

_____

_____

_____

_____

_____

_____

_____

Self care
Is Not
Selfish

Sexy Baby Mama
Self-Reflections

I practiced Self-Care today by:

My support system consists of:

I Feel:

☐ Supported
☐ Protected
☐ Happy
☐ Excited
☐ Optimistic
☐ Overwhelmed
☐ In Love
☐ Sad
☐ Angry
☐ Scared

Self care Is Not Selfish

Sexy Baby Mama
Self-Reflections

I practiced Self-Care today by:

My support system consists of:

I Feel:

☐ Supported
☐ Protected
☐ Happy
☐ Excited
☐ Optimistic
☐ Overwhelmed
☐ In Love
☐ Sad
☐ Angry
☐ Scared

Self care
Is Not
Selfish

Sexy Baby Mama
Self-Reflections

Today's Date:
_____

I practiced Self-Care today by:

My support system consists of:

I Feel:

- ☐ Supported
- ☐ Protected
- ☐ Happy
- ☐ Excited
- ☐ Optimistic
- ☐ Overwhelmed
- ☐ In Love
- ☐ Sad
- ☐ Angry
- ☐ Scared

Self care
Is Not
Selfish

Sexy Baby Mama
Self-Reflections

I practiced Self-Care today by:

My support system consists of:

I Feel:

☐ Supported
☐ Protected
☐ Happy
☐ Excited
☐ Optimistic
☐ Overwhelmed
☐ In Love
☐ Sad
☐ Angry
☐ Scared

Self care
Is Not
Selfish

Sexy Baby Mama
Self-Reflections

I practiced Self-Care today by:

My support system consists of:

I Feel:

☐ Supported
☐ Protected
☐ Happy
☐ Excited
☐ Optimistic
☐ Overwhelmed
☐ In Love
☐ Sad
☐ Angry
☐ Scared

_____
_____
_____
_____
_____
_____
_____
_____
_____
_____
_____
_____
_____
_____
_____
_____
_____
_____

Self care
Is Not
Selfish

Sexy Baby Mama
Self-Reflections

I practiced Self-Care today by:

My support system consists of:

I Feel:

☐ Supported
☐ Protected
☐ Happy
☐ Excited
☐ Optimistic
☐ Overwhelmed
☐ In Love
☐ Sad
☐ Angry
☐ Scared

Self care
Is Not
Selfish

Sexy Baby Mama
Self-Reflections

_____

I practiced Self-Care today by:

My support system consists of:

I Feel:

☐ Supported
☐ Protected
☐ Happy
☐ Excited
☐ Optimistic
☐ Overwhelmed
☐ In Love
☐ Sad
☐ Angry
☐ Scared

Self care
Is Not
Selfish

Sexy Baby Mama
Self-Reflections

I practiced Self-Care today by:

My support system consists of:

I Feel:

☐ Supported
☐ Protected
☐ Happy
☐ Excited
☐ Optimistic
☐ Overwhelmed
☐ In Love
☐ Sad
☐ Angry
☐ Scared

Self-care
Is Not
Selfish

Sexy Baby Mama
Self-Reflections

I practiced Self-Care today by:

My support system consists of:

I Feel:

- ☐ Supported
- ☐ Protected
- ☐ Happy
- ☐ Excited
- ☐ Optimistic
- ☐ Overwhelmed
- ☐ In Love
- ☐ Sad
- ☐ Angry
- ☐ Scared

Self care Is Not Selfish

Sexy Baby Mama
Self-Reflections

I practiced Self-Care today by:

My support system consists of:

I Feel:

☐ Supported
☐ Protected
☐ Happy
☐ Excited
☐ Optimistic
☐ Overwhelmed
☐ In Love
☐ Sad
☐ Angry
☐ Scared

Self care
Is Not
Selfish

Sexy Baby Mama
Self-Reflections

I practiced Self-Care today by:

My support system consists of:

I Feel:

☐ Supported
☐ Protected
☐ Happy
☐ Excited
☐ Optimistic
☐ Overwhelmed
☐ In Love
☐ Sad
☐ Angry
☐ Scared

Self-care Is Not Selfish

Sexy Baby Mama
Self-Reflections

_____

I practiced Self-Care today by:

My support system consists of:

I Feel:

☐ Supported
☐ Protected
☐ Happy
☐ Excited
☐ Optimistic
☐ Overwhelmed
☐ In Love
☐ Sad
☐ Angry
☐ Scared

Self care
Is Not
Selfish

Sexy Baby Mama
Self-Reflections

I practiced Self-Care today by:

My support system consists of:

I Feel:

- ☐ Supported
- ☐ Protected
- ☐ Happy
- ☐ Excited
- ☐ Optimistic
- ☐ Overwhelmed
- ☐ In Love
- ☐ Sad
- ☐ Angry
- ☐ Scared

Self care Is Not Selfish

Sexy Baby Mama
Self-Reflections

_____

I practiced Self-Care today by:

My support system consists of:

I Feel:

☐ Supported
☐ Protected
☐ Happy
☐ Excited
☐ Optimistic
☐ Overwhelmed
☐ In Love
☐ Sad
☐ Angry
☐ Scared

Self-care
Is Not
Selfish

97

Sexy Baby Mama
Self-Reflections

I practiced Self-Care today by:

My support system consists of:

I Feel:

- ☐ Supported
- ☐ Protected
- ☐ Happy
- ☐ Excited
- ☐ Optimistic
- ☐ Overwhelmed
- ☐ In Love
- ☐ Sad
- ☐ Angry
- ☐ Scared

Self care Is Not Selfish

Sexy Baby Mama
Self-Reflections

I practiced Self-Care today by:

My support system consists of:

I Feel:

- ☐ Supported
- ☐ Protected
- ☐ Happy
- ☐ Excited
- ☐ Optimistic
- ☐ Overwhelmed
- ☐ In Love
- ☐ Sad
- ☐ Angry
- ☐ Scared

Self care
Is Not
Selfish

Sexy Baby Mama
Self-Reflections

_____

I practiced Self-Care today by:

My support system consists of:

I Feel:

☐ Supported
☐ Protected
☐ Happy
☐ Excited
☐ Optimistic
☐ Overwhelmed
☐ In Love
☐ Sad
☐ Angry
☐ Scared

_____
_____
_____
_____
_____
_____
_____
_____
_____
_____
_____
_____
_____
_____
_____
_____
_____
_____
_____
_____

Self care
Is Not
Selfish

Sexy Baby Mama
Self-Reflections

I practiced Self-Care today by:

My support system consists of:

I Feel:

☐ Supported
☐ Protected
☐ Happy
☐ Excited
☐ Optimistic
☐ Overwhelmed
☐ In Love
☐ Sad
☐ Angry
☐ Scared

Self care
Is Not
Selfish

Sexy Baby Mama
Self-Reflections

I practiced Self-Care today by:

My support system consists of:

I Feel:

☐ Supported
☐ Protected
☐ Happy
☐ Excited
☐ Optimistic
☐ Overwhelmed
☐ In Love
☐ Sad
☐ Angry
☐ Scared

Self-care Is Not Selfish

Sexy Baby Mama
Self-Reflections

I practiced Self-Care today by:

My support system consists of:

I Feel:

☐ Supported
☐ Protected
☐ Happy
☐ Excited
☐ Optimistic
☐ Overwhelmed
☐ In Love
☐ Sad
☐ Angry
☐ Scared

Self care
Is Not
Selfish

Sexy Baby Mama
Self-Reflections

I practiced Self-Care today by:

My support system consists of:

I Feel:

- ☐ Supported
- ☐ Protected
- ☐ Happy
- ☐ Excited
- ☐ Optimistic
- ☐ Overwhelmed
- ☐ In Love
- ☐ Sad
- ☐ Angry
- ☐ Scared

Self care
Is Not
Selfish

Sexy Baby Mama
Self-Reflections

Today's Date:
_____

I practiced Self-Care today by:

My support system consists of:

I Feel:

☐ Supported
☐ Protected
☐ Happy
☐ Excited
☐ Optimistic
☐ Overwhelmed
☐ In Love
☐ Sad
☐ Angry
☐ Scared

Self care
Is Not
Selfish

Sexy Baby Mama
Self-Reflections

I practiced Self-Care today by:

My support system consists of:

I Feel:

☐ Supported
☐ Protected
☐ Happy
☐ Excited
☐ Optimistic
☐ Overwhelmed
☐ In Love
☐ Sad
☐ Angry
☐ Scared

Self care Is Not Selfish

Sexy Baby Mama
Self-Reflections

I practiced Self-Care today by:

My support system consists of:

I Feel:

☐ Supported
☐ Protected
☐ Happy
☐ Excited
☐ Optimistic
☐ Overwhelmed
☐ In Love
☐ Sad
☐ Angry
☐ Scared

_____

_____

_____

_____

_____

_____

_____

_____

_____

_____

_____

_____

_____

_____

_____

_____

_____

_____

_____

_____

Self care
Is Not
Selfish

Sexy Baby Mama
Self-Reflections

I practiced Self-Care today by:

My support system consists of:

I Feel:

☐ Supported
☐ Protected
☐ Happy
☐ Excited
☐ Optimistic
☐ Overwhelmed
☐ In Love
☐ Sad
☐ Angry
☐ Scared

Self-care Is Not Selfish

Sexy Baby Mama
Self-Reflections

I practiced Self-Care today by:

My support system consists of:

I Feel:

☐ Supported
☐ Protected
☐ Happy
☐ Excited
☐ Optimistic
☐ Overwhelmed
☐ In Love
☐ Sad
☐ Angry
☐ Scared

Self-care
Is Not
Selfish

Sexy Baby Mama
Self-Reflections

I practiced Self-Care today by:

My support system consists of:

I Feel:

☐ Supported
☐ Protected
☐ Happy
☐ Excited
☐ Optimistic
☐ Overwhelmed
☐ In Love
☐ Sad
☐ Angry
☐ Scared

Self care
Is Not
Selfish

Sexy Baby Mama
Self-Reflections

I practiced Self-Care today by:

My support system consists of:

I Feel:

☐ Supported
☐ Protected
☐ Happy
☐ Excited
☐ Optimistic
☐ Overwhelmed
☐ In Love
☐ Sad
☐ Angry
☐ Scared

Self care Is Not Selfish

Sexy Baby Mama
Self-Reflections

I practiced Self-Care today by:

My support system consists of:

I Feel:

- ☐ Supported
- ☐ Protected
- ☐ Happy
- ☐ Excited
- ☐ Optimistic
- ☐ Overwhelmed
- ☐ In Love
- ☐ Sad
- ☐ Angry
- ☐ Scared

Self care Is Not Selfish

Sexy Baby Mama
Self-Reflections

I practiced Self-Care today by:

My support system consists of:

I Feel:

☐ Supported
☐ Protected
☐ Happy
☐ Excited
☐ Optimistic
☐ Overwhelmed
☐ In Love
☐ Sad
☐ Angry
☐ Scared

_____

_____

_____

_____

_____

_____

_____

_____

_____

_____

_____

_____

_____

_____

_____

_____

_____

_____

Self care
Is Not
Selfish

Sexy Baby Mama
Self-Reflections

I practiced Self-Care today by:

My support system consists of:

I Feel:

- ☐ Supported
- ☐ Protected
- ☐ Happy
- ☐ Excited
- ☐ Optimistic
- ☐ Overwhelmed
- ☐ In Love
- ☐ Sad
- ☐ Angry
- ☐ Scared

Self care
Is Not
Selfish

Sexy Baby Mama
Self-Reflections

I practiced Self-Care today by:
My support system consists of:

I Feel:

- ☐ Supported
- ☐ Protected
- ☐ Happy
- ☐ Excited
- ☐ Optimistic
- ☐ Overwhelmed
- ☐ In Love
- ☐ Sad
- ☐ Angry
- ☐ Scared

Self care
Is Not
Selfish

Sexy Baby Mama
Self-Reflections

I practiced Self-Care today by:

My support system consists of:

I Feel:

- ☐ Supported
- ☐ Protected
- ☐ Happy
- ☐ Excited
- ☐ Optimistic
- ☐ Overwhelmed
- ☐ In Love
- ☐ Sad
- ☐ Angry
- ☐ Scared

Self care
Is Not
Selfish

Sexy Baby Mama
Self-Reflections

I practiced Self-Care today by:

My support system consists of:

I Feel:

☐ Supported
☐ Protected
☐ Happy
☐ Excited
☐ Optimistic
☐ Overwhelmed
☐ In Love
☐ Sad
☐ Angry
☐ Scared

Self-care
Is Not
Selfish

Sexy Baby Mama
Self-Reflections

Today's Date:
_____

I practiced Self-Care today by:

My support system consists of:

I Feel:

☐ Supported
☐ Protected
☐ Happy
☐ Excited
☐ Optimistic
☐ Overwhelmed
☐ In Love
☐ Sad
☐ Angry
☐ Scared

Self care
Is Not
Selfish

118

Sexy Baby Mama
Self-Reflections

I practiced Self-Care today by:

My support system consists of:

I Feel:

☐ Supported
☐ Protected
☐ Happy
☐ Excited
☐ Optimistic
☐ Overwhelmed
☐ In Love
☐ Sad
☐ Angry
☐ Scared

Self care
Is Not
Selfish

Sexy Baby Mama
Self-Reflections

_____

I practiced Self-Care today by:

My support system consists of:

I Feel:

☐ Supported
☐ Protected
☐ Happy
☐ Excited
☐ Optimistic
☐ Overwhelmed
☐ In Love
☐ Sad
☐ Angry
☐ Scared

_____
_____
_____
_____
_____
_____
_____
_____
_____
_____
_____
_____
_____
_____
_____
_____
_____
_____

Self care
Is Not
Selfish

Sexy Baby Mama
Self-Reflections

I practiced Self-Care today by:

My support system consists of:

I Feel:

☐ Supported
☐ Protected
☐ Happy
☐ Excited
☐ Optimistic
☐ Overwhelmed
☐ In Love
☐ Sad
☐ Angry
☐ Scared

Self care Is Not Selfish

Sexy Baby Mama
Self-Reflections

I practiced Self-Care today by:

My support system consists of:

I Feel:

☐ Supported
☐ Protected
☐ Happy
☐ Excited
☐ Optimistic
☐ Overwhelmed
☐ In Love
☐ Sad
☐ Angry
☐ Scared

Self care
Is Not
Selfish

Sexy Baby Mama
Self-Reflections

I practiced Self-Care today by:

My support system consists of:

I Feel:

☐ Supported
☐ Protected
☐ Happy
☐ Excited
☐ Optimistic
☐ Overwhelmed
☐ In Love
☐ Sad
☐ Angry
☐ Scared

Self care
Is Not
Selfish

Sexy Baby Mama
Self-Reflections

I practiced Self-Care today by:

My support system consists of:

I Feel:

- ☐ Supported
- ☐ Protected
- ☐ Happy
- ☐ Excited
- ☐ Optimistic
- ☐ Overwhelmed
- ☐ In Love
- ☐ Sad
- ☐ Angry
- ☐ Scared

_____
_____
_____
_____
_____
_____
_____
_____
_____
_____
_____
_____
_____
_____
_____
_____
_____

Self care
Is Not
Selfish

Sexy Baby Mama
Self-Reflections

I practiced Self-Care today by:

My support system consists of:

I Feel:

☐ Supported
☐ Protected
☐ Happy
☐ Excited
☐ Optimistic
☐ Overwhelmed
☐ In Love
☐ Sad
☐ Angry
☐ Scared

Self care
Is Not
Selfish

Kinyatta E. Gray is a Best-Selling Author, Travel Influencer and the CEO of FlightsInStilettos, LLC. Kinyatta is also the Chief Beach Towel Designer for the FlightsInStilettos Glam Girl Beach Towels.

Websites:

https://www.flightsinstilettos.com/

https://www.kinyattagray.com/

https://www.honoringmissbee.com/